Love Poems for Michael II

by

Joan McNerney

ISBN: 978-93-6354-930-2

First Edition: 2024
Rs. 200/-

Cyberwit.net
HIG 45 Kaushambi Kunj, Kalindipuram
Allahabad - 211011 (U.P.) India
http://www.cyberwit.net
Tel: +(91) 9415091004
E-mail: info@cyberwit.net

Printed at Repro India Limited.

INTRODUCTION

New England is the home of dazzling autumns. Trees become vivid rainbows as each day more colors emerge. Then an even more spectacular season arrives called winter. Snow gusts fly over heaven like wings of angels.

Lovers will hide away from frost and mighty winds. This is my story of autumn and winter romance in the Northeast.

Contents

It's Sunday

Your laughter comes
in cascades when I toss
your curly hair, tickling those
big ears with blades of grass.

We stop at the lake startling
frogs just before they leap
away and listen to squirrels
brushing over crunchy leaves.

You turn to hold me hold me.
Hurry it's late. O Michael,
clouds ribbon heaven and I want
your arms around me forever.

Indian Summer

Four sparkling maples
sashaying in fall winds.
dressed in yellow lace.

We hear children kicking
up leaves shouting, jumping
over mounds of foliage.

Bright leaves gleaming
in sunshine tumbling
through an Alice blue sky.

Carpets of red yellow brown
foliage unfurl before us.

Strolling through trails of trees
becoming spellbound by
leafy giants towering above.

For a moment we will rest
waiting for evening to
cover the sky as shadows
touch your face.

Our Hideaway

That weepy September
marigolds were so full.
Do you remember?

Mixing with rain, leaves
make streets slippery.
I was careful not to slip,
dreading when they would
grow dry and crumble.

Foliage begins to droop
too ripe and heavy for
trees. Some live all winter
through the next spring.
Chased by winds, they
huddle in corners,
reminding me of mice.

Revealing my childhood
possessed by rosaries
and nuns chanting Ave,
Ave, Ave Maria...
I confessed to you
how I loved Russian
poets and waited for
a silent revolution.

You proclaim my navel exudes
the warmth of 10,000 suns
and my eyes are two big
bunches of morning glories.

I reply with an embrace.

Autumn Days

Morning light reveals
silhouettes of branches
against a dove gray sky.

Wearing layers of red orange
yellow…trees begin dancing,
double stepping in the wind.

Now it's time to gather lots of
bright vegetables. I'll cook
pots of soup, yeasty breads.

Countless shades of leaves,
shapes of leaves spreading
over a lingering sunset.

Half moon hiding in old
oak tree on top of a hillside.

We're On Our Way

Winds whistling through
an old blue truck. Our dog
barking out directions.

How many plans we had.
We'd live off the fat
of the land. Just put
your finger on the map
and off we would roll.

Stopping by the road side
for coffee and muffins. I want
to taste your sweet neck.

Your name is always
on my lips only you,
Michael, only you.

Proclamation

I love you and I'll
shout it from rooftops.
Chisel giant hearts
through Mount Everest.
Take out an entire edition
of the New York Times.

You love me and you'll
preempt the president.
Send our rocket to Venus.
Fly fluorescent banners
over the United Nations.

Let's write our names
on this perfect sky
so even heaven knows
we are in love.

Love's Equation

Hope the phone bill isn't too high.
All Michael did last week was
call me from out of town.

Today he finally came home
with three red roses, I made him
six blueberry muffins.

For hours we kissed touching
his mouth with my tongue...
my electric tongue.

I put his two suitcases away
telling him to please be careful
with my clean floor.

Maybe one million times
I've told that man not to
make such as mess!

After twenty years, who's counting?

Blizzard

We woke up to a wonderful
emergency announced on
abrupt radio reports.

Silver needles spun for hours
weaving tapestries to drape
rooftops, sidewalks, streets.

Millions of icicles delicately
arranged on metal railings
around cornices.

White magic prayed by children.
A trance shutting down school
making way for snow fights.

Now we have some extra time
to snuggle longer in bed. Stay
warm together. Be late for work.

Snow crystals cover all stains
and blemishes. Our glass
panes become miniature
museums of fine line etchings.

We are snapped awake by frost.
Our woolen gloves full of lace.

Wintertime

Hurry, short days are here,
too much to do.
Get ready, find gloves
hats scarves sweaters.

Stopping to see the
shape of a snowflake

Coming home to luxuriate
in dim light listening
to heat hissing and finding
warmth from hot teas

Bundled in bed comforted by
mounds of blankets, books.

We finally succumb to
our northern goddess
whose black nights are long
and silent as evergreens.

Now we can count up how
many stars fit in our window
as we whisper sweet nothings.

Present

You gave me five brown pods
to grow in my garden bed.

Five brown pods to grow...
night blooms of wisteria.

I put them in a glass jar
with my golden locket.

Five brown pods winding
through heaven.

Weaving night with winter
wishes for wisteria.

In a flower dress wandering
over perfumed fields.

I sleepwalk searching for my
locket and your caress.

Lying Around

In our love nest
watching snow gather.
You say it's not as
pretty as I am.

Unloosening my clothes
throwing them and everything
else from the bed. Warmer warmer
we want our time together.

When the moon is full
faces of frost cover
our window. We will
nestle asleep while storms
drift past the night.

Wintry Bouquet

This December
during wide nights
hemmed by blackness,
we remember roses.
Pink yellow red violet
those satin blooms of June.

We must wait six months
before seeing blossoms,
touch their brightness
crush their scent
with fingertips.

Now there are only
ebony pools of winter's
heavy ink of darkness.

Dipping into memory of
our lips touching petals,
those tantalizing sweet buds.

We glimpse brilliant faces of
flowers right before us.
Burrowing beneath warm blankets.
Bracing against that long, cold
nocturnal of wind and shadow.

Tonight

Boughs build archways as tips
of trees touch each other. What
was shaded green becomes
nocturnal shadow.

A crescent moon hangs from
heaven. Light tracing
foliage falls dropping
dusty deep upon ground.

Secrets lie inside edged shadows.
Animals hide under darkness
resounding through night
as leaves rustle.

Our sky is embroidered with
stars born from nebulous clouds.
Clouds roam across heaven
drifting through an airy dance.

Blue starlight glides over black
horizon. Cosmic butterflies.

Surprise!

Finding another love note
hidden in my calendar.

There are too many calendars
and too many clocks.
There is never enough time.
We must save this minute.

This minute of mercury
this velvet night as sleepless
stars glide through the sky
in aerial ballet.

You remind me of the
milky way, luminous bands
of light moving over heaven.
All on fire. Your fingers
hot to touch.

You remind of the
milky way, brighter
each and every second.
We speed across green
comets. All seven spheres
to explore playing catch
with pulsars.

Let's sneak some
kisses under Venus
now.

Blue Skies

After autumn's golden splendor
our world is dressed in wintry frost
sparkling though long nights.

Bright green springtime awakens
diamond raindrops as shafts of
sunlight burst open summer's glory.

We will always remember how
many blue skies we shared together
during these four seasons of our love.

www.ingramcontent.com/pod-product-compliance
Lightning Source LLC
LaVergne TN
LVHW041306150826
845673LV00008B/2762